JOHN BAKER | JOHNNY BAKER
MAC OWEN

Celebrate Recovery®
28 Devotions

HEALING FROM HURTS, HABITS, AND HANG-UPS

Celebrate Recovery® booklet
© 2016 by John Baker, Johnny Baker, and Mac Owen

Requests for information should be addressed to: Zondervan, 3900 Sparks
Dr., SE, Grand Rapids, MI 49546

Unless otherwise noted, Scripture quotations are taken from the Holy Bible,
New International Version®, NIV®. Copyright © 1973, 1978, 1984 by Biblica,
Inc.® Used by permission of Zondervan. All rights reserved worldwide. www.
zondervan.com. The "NIV" and "New International Version" are trademarks
registered in the United States Patent and Trademark Office by Biblica, Inc.®
Scripture quotations marked NKJV are from the New King James Version®.
© 1982 by Thomas Nelson. Used by permission. All rights reserved.

Cover design: Kristy Edwards

ISBN 978-0-3103-6032-2

Printed in the United States of America

17 18 19 20 POL 23 22 21 20 19 18 17 16 15 14 13 12 11 10 9 8 7 6 5

Then they cried out to the LORD in their trouble,

And He saved them out of their distresses.

He sent His word and healed them,

And delivered them from their destructions.

Oh, that men would give thanks to

the LORD for His goodness,

And for His wonderful works

to the children of men!

PSALM 107:19–21 NKJV

The First Step

I know that nothing good lives in me, that is,
in my sinful nature. For I have the desire to do
what is good, but I cannot carry it out.

ROMANS 7:18

No one gets to start in the middle—we're all beginners in one area of our lives or another. But for many of us, what we need is more like a new beginning, a fresh start, a walking journey from chaos to wholeness that is accomplished one step at a time. We call that journey "recovery." Let's look at that first step:

Step 1: We admitted we were powerless over our
addictions and compulsive behaviors. That our lives
had become unmanageable.

Our first step is a big one. We are finally ready to admit that we are powerless to control an addiction or a behavior. The harder we try, the more unmanageable it becomes. Our lives have descended into chaos. When we take that first big step—giving up control—we are stepping away from denial and acknowledging our own need.

There is hope in that first step, for we can't be helped until we admit that we need help. Until then we are trying to be God in our own lives, and really we just aren't up to the task. We are powerless to control much of anything by our own power. Step 1 allows us to find freedom from ourselves.

PRAYER

Father God, today I take that first important step toward healing and wholeness. I admit to you that I'm powerless over the strongholds that have taken over my life. I desperately need your help. In Jesus' name, Amen.

What Is Freedom?

*"You will know the truth, and the
truth will make you free."*

JOHN 8:32 NCV

Many years ago when I was in the service, the Fourth of July was approaching. It was the job of my squadron's safety officer to develop a slogan and put up posters discouraging drinking over the holiday weekend.

We had no accidents that year, and it was attributed partly to the slogan this guy came up with: "He who comes forth with a fifth on the fourth may not come forth on the fifth."

What comes to mind when you hear the words Fourth of July? Independence Day? The Declaration of Independence? World War II? When I think of the Fourth of July, I think of freedom. But what is true freedom?

Abraham Lincoln said, "Those who deny freedom to others deserve it not for themselves, and, under a just God, cannot long retain it." And we have all heard the great quote from Patrick Henry, "Give me liberty or give me death." But, here again, what is true liberty?

The basic test of freedom is not in what we are free to do but rather in what we are free *not* to do! Today, I am free not to drink! For me that's a very precious freedom.

PRAYER

Heavenly Father, I want to celebrate freedom in my life. Help me to openly and honestly deal with those things that take away my freedom to live in a manner that pleases you. In Jesus' name, Amen.

Change Is Possible

*Outwardly we are wasting away, yet inwardly
we are being renewed day by day.*

2 CORINTHIANS 4:16

Some words are like oxygen to my soul: "I was struggling in hopelessness but now have hope." "God is changing me." "I could not have made it through this storm without Christ." "I have a new family for life now." "I have learned so much about myself, and for the first time, I like what I see." "I am now the spouse I know I was called to be." "My relationship with my kids is growing healthier!"

There is nothing sweeter than seeing life change up close and personal. None of us is "fixed" but one thing is for sure: growth and change are becoming daily realities in so many lives. God has lifted me up and taught me some incredible lessons, even through times of hurt and pain. It has been said, "You can forgive what hurt you in the past. Just never forget what it taught you."

When we get to that place of surrender where we can

say to God, "I'm tired of doing this on my own," then we can begin the process of allowing him to change us. No matter what we find ourselves in the middle of, no matter what poor choices we've made, no matter what struggles and hurts we've experienced, God still loves us and desires to comfort, protect, and guide us out of our mess and pain. In the process, he teaches us how to live more fruitfully.

PRAYER

Lord in heaven, thank you for teaching me even through the hurt and pain in my life. In Jesus' name, Amen.

The Second Step

*It is God who works in you to will and to
act according to his good purpose.*

PHILIPPIANS 2:13

The admission that we are powerless over an addiction or compulsive behavior in our lives opens us up to reach out to God. We begin to understand that he wants to fill our lives with his love, his joy, his hope, and his presence. That first step turned our eyes away from ourselves as the source of healing, and the second step turns our eyes toward God.

Step 2: We came to believe that a power greater than ourselves could restore us to sanity.

If we can't heal ourselves, then who can we turn to for help? God is the only one who has the power to exchange our chaos for freedom. Of course, he knew long before we did what would be needed. He sent Jesus to save us from sin and sickness. He sent his power player to earth, someone who was tempted as we are in all ways but without sin. He is not just a higher power. He is the highest power, because he has conquered all life can dish out. He did that for us so we could imagine freedom from sin in our own lives.

What freedom it brings to know that when we are powerless, we have an ally to help us through the hard times—and all the times are hard, aren't they?

PRAYER

Heavenly Father, I've made such a mess of things. I'm so grateful that you care for me and came to show me the way out of chaos and into freedom. In Jesus' name, Amen.

A Picture of Redemption

*"If you do what is right, will not you be accepted? But
if you do not do what is right, sin is crouching at your
door; it desires to have you, but you must master it."*

GENESIS 4:7

Every once in a while God gives us the chance to witness a miracle! Recently, a leader in Celebrate Recovery shared this miracle with me:

"A year ago a man walked into my office, broken, at his wit's end, with a heart full of despair. He was angry and trying to cope with a host of substances and other unhealthy habits that were destroying his mind and hardening his heart. He was ready to abandon his wife and family. Last night I saw this man again at a Celebrate Recovery graduation service. Now, eleven months sober, he is a completely different man.

"With tears in his eyes, he accepted his 12-Step chip and then expressed his love for his wife who was sitting close by. I was humbled as I heard him talk about the restoration that had come to his marriage and how his kids are rejoicing and talking about God. He then quoted the following Bible passage, changing *you* to *I*: 'If I do what is right, will not I be accepted? But if I do not do what is right, sin is crouching at my door; it desires to have me, but I must master it.'

"The man I met a year ago is no more. In his place, a new leader has been born. That's what I call a true miracle—the transformation of a human life."

PRAYER

Dear God of miracles, I stand in awe of what you have done in so many lives. My words cannot express your greatness. In Jesus' name, Amen.

Celebrate Your Recovery

*You turned my wailing into dancing; you removed
my sackcloth and clothed me with joy, that my
heart may sing your praises and not be silent.
LORD my God, I will praise you forever.*

PSALM 30:11–12

Have you ever wondered why Celebrate Recovery is called *Celebrate* Recovery? Well . . . people usually seek help when things are bad. Which means none of us has much to celebrate when we first enter the program. That isn't always the case, of course, but usually people begin coming to Celebrate Recovery when things are far from ideal.

But soon, God begins to change things. He takes our pain and gives us purpose. He takes our crying and turns it into praise. He gives us joy and peace and freedom from our hurts, hang-ups, and habits. He gives us reason to celebrate.

Of course, it doesn't happen all at once. There will still be days when we hurt, feel stuck, or don't believe there is much to celebrate. There are sure to be hard times in recovery—pain we have to face, amends we have to make, forgiveness we must offer. But for those who hold on, there is hope and healing. There is reason to celebrate!

The important thing to remember is that we must hold fast to our commitment. We must refuse to quit. Each day we actively work toward our recovery, we will be able to thank God and share our testimony with someone who needs to hear it. Each day, we come one step closer to complete healing for our lives.

PRAYER

Father, I feel stuck right now. Please give me the resolve to continue to seek recovery. In Jesus' name, Amen.

The Third Step

Therefore, I urge you, brothers, in view of God's mercy, to offer your bodies as living sacrifices, holy and pleasing to God—this is your spiritual act of worship.

ROMANS 12:1

One step at a time—that's how it's done! In the first step, we acknowledged that we were powerless over our addictions and compulsive behaviors. In Step 2, we came to believe that there is a power greater than ourselves who loves us and wants to restore us to wholeness. Those first two steps were so important they established a cause for action. Step 3 is our first action step.

Step 3: We made a decision to turn our lives and our wills over to the care of God.

God has given each of us a precious gift: the freedom to choose. It was a risky proposition for him. He wanted us to choose good but knew we might choose evil. He wanted us to choose life, but what if we chose death? He wanted us to choose freedom but knew we might choose addiction. Still, it was a risk he was willing to take so that he would know this: when we ask him into our lives, it is because we have freely chosen to have him there.

The third step offers us the opportunity to choose to surrender our lives to God, an opportunity to choose freedom over our self-will, which always falls short of God's mark for us.

PRAYER

Lord God, thank you for giving me the power to choose. I see that it is a wonderful gift. Help me use it in a way that is pleasing to you. In Jesus' name, Amen.

Forgiving Others

*Be kind and compassionate to one another, forgiving
each other, just as in Christ God forgave you.*

EPHESIANS 4:32

It isn't easy to forgive those who have hurt us. It feels
wrong somehow, like we're perverting justice, letting
those off the hook who deserve to pay for their actions.
Looking at it another way, though, don't we want others to
forgive us quickly when we do the wrong thing and harm
someone in the process?

Jesus Christ is the greatest of all forgivers. He went
to the cross and paid the debt for our sins, so that now
we have been declared "not guilty." The Bible says that
remembering how much we've been forgiven will always
make the forgiveness process easier. Christ did not per-
vert justice, but he satisfied it in its purest and most perfect
state.

Like he always does, God teaches us, his children, by
example. He knew we would struggle to forgive because
our human nature is primarily self-serving. He knew the

only way for us to free ourselves and others from the burden of unforgiveness would be to demonstrate it in a most spectacular way. When we remind ourselves what Jesus did, we can better accept what we must do.

<hr>

PRAYER

Father, thank you for the forgiveness you have poured out on me. It is unearned in every way. Thank you for not giving me the pure justice I once thought I wanted. In Jesus' name, Amen.

The Fourth Step

Let us examine our ways and test them,
and let us return to the LORD.

LAMENTATIONS 3:40

Now that our feet are moving, we're ready to get to work. The fourth step begins the cleanup process. In Steps 2 and 3, we assessed our condition, made changes in our thinking, and decided to surrender our lives to God, our Higher Power. To use a simple analogy, we have discovered and acknowledged that we have tooth decay. We have decided to do something about it, and now we are ready to start chipping away at the decay brought on by our past mistakes. This decay has built up over the years and kept us from seeing the truth about our past and present situations.

Step 4: We made a searching and fearless moral
inventory of ourselves.

The fourth step requires us to free ourselves from denial and face our secrets. As we chip away at the decay, we are faced with the truth about ourselves and others. It can be frightening, unsettling, uncomfortable, but God doesn't expect us to go through it alone. Because we've invited him, he is there with us, whispering words of comfort and encouragement.

We've come a long way already, and we've learned that every step is a victory in and of itself. Recovery is tough because it requires us to face harsh truths, but the truth always sets us free.

PRAYER

Father, I want to be free to serve you with all my heart and soul and mind, but I'm afraid of what lies ahead on the path. Thank you for your promise never to leave me. In Jesus' name, Amen.

The Trouble with Grudges

*"Forgive us our debts, as we also have forgiven
our debtors. And lead us not into temptation,
but deliver us from the evil one."*

MATTHEW 6:12–13

The only possible way we could avoid being hurt by others would be to live completely alone. As long as there is more than one person, hurts will happen. They are the cutting edge of every relationship. We can't keep ourselves from getting hurt from time to time, but we can control our reactions. And that is seriously important.

One of the ways we often react to hurt is by bottling up the resentment until it becomes a grudge. We reason that as long as we hold on to that hurt, the person who hurt us isn't getting away with it. Unfortunately, those who hurt us are often unaware, and we end up harboring a grudge that only keeps us from healing.

Revenge is another way we might react to being hurt. We feel sure that getting even, hurting back as much as

we've been hurt, will relieve the pain and satisfy our long-
ing for justice. Instead, revenge just poisons our souls and
keeps us focused on the past.

The only sure way to get rid of a hurt is to forgive the
one who hurt us. By forgiving, we call the debt settled, and
it no longer has power over our lives. No wonder God asks
us to forgive. He knows it will always be for our good.

PRAYER

*Thank you for helping me to forgive those who have hurt
me. I can see that holding grudges and seeking revenge
only keep me anchored to the past. In Jesus' name, Amen.*

Hitting Bottom

*"Come to me, all you who are weary and
burdened, and I will give you rest."*

MATTHEW 11:28

A few months ago, someone told me, "I'm ready to hit bottom. When will I get there?" This is how I answered: "When you stop digging!" It's simple, really. We hit bottom when we finally get tired of being beat up by ourselves and others. Then and only then, at the point of complete surrender, do we find rest. This isn't the sitting and doing nothing kind of rest—it's peace of mind.

Peace of mind is the greatest rest of all. But before we can get there, we have to wave the white flag and say, "I give up!" It's not easy, but there are a few things that can help you. First, surround yourself with people who are having victories and making progress in their recovery and in their lives. Second, stop digging your hole deeper by flooding your thoughts with the bad thinking that has gotten you where you are. Third, fill your mind with good things by memorizing Scripture and reading encouraging books.

Peace of mind is attainable, but it requires a new lifestyle, new habits, new behaviors, and new relationships that are strong and upright. With God's help, we can all find our way, but nothing less than complete commitment will get us there.

PRAYER

Father, I want peace of mind. I have been a captive to my painful, troubling, disobedient thoughts for far too long. As I surrender to you, surround myself with good people, and flood my mind with your Word, I pray that you will bring me the gift of peace. In Jesus' name, Amen.

The Fifth Step

*Therefore confess your sins to each other and
pray for each other so that you may be healed.*

JAMES 5:16

As soon as we confess our sins to God, we experience his forgiveness. Being free from the penalty of our sins and living in fellowship with God is true freedom and more than we could have ever thought or imagined. But our loving, generous God has given us more—the love and support of our brothers and sisters in Christ.

*Step 5: We admitted to God, to ourselves, and to
another human being the exact nature of our wrongs.*

In recovery we hear, time and time again, that we are only as sick as our secrets. In Step 5, we discover we are free to share those secrets in a safe place, with safe people. We learn that this is not a journey to be taken alone—that we need others in our recovery to support us, pray for us, and encourage us.

Of course, we should choose wisely before confessing our past sins to others. But I'm confident that God has placed people in each of our lives who are willing to respect our confidences and support us as we move toward healing. Celebrate Recovery was formed to provide that kind of confidentiality and support. God knows exactly what we need to complete our journey to wholeness.

PRAYER

Thank you, Lord, for understanding my need for brothers and sisters in the faith who can strengthen and support me as I share my secrets and walk toward wholeness. In Jesus' name, Amen.

One Day at a Time

I urge you, brothers and sisters, in view of God's mercy, to
offer your bodies as a living sacrifice, holy and pleasing
to God—this is your true and proper worship.

ROMANS 12:1

Most of us don't seek help until we realize that something is out of control in our lives. Sometimes another person realizes it for us, but either way, we come looking for help in an area that obviously needs attention. After we've been in recovery for a while, however, it becomes clear that flaws in our character may have been what got us into big trouble in the first place. If we don't deal with them, they will keep us from living a life fully committed to Christ.

The bad news is that we all have these character flaws. No one is perfect. Maybe we are people pleasers, or we have anger issues. We might feel we have to spend money to feel good about ourselves, or we use food to stuff our emotions. We may have control issues. Whatever the case, these character flaws are always at the root of our big problems.

It's important to acknowledge these character flaws and offer them to God. We start with the big issue, the one causing us the most pain, and then we begin working on all the smaller areas God reveals to us. The process works because God is in it. All we need to do is acknowledge the need for change, offer ourselves to him, and then work alongside him while he works those things out in our lives.

PRAYER

Thank you, Lord, for helping me to see the flaws behind my failings. With your help, I will face them one day at a time. In Jesus' name, Amen.

Jesus Wept

*When Jesus saw her weeping, and the Jews who had
come along with her also weeping, he was deeply moved
in spirit and troubled, "Where have you laid him?" he
asked. "Come and see, Lord," they replied. Jesus wept.*

JOHN 11:33–35

When we enter recovery, surrendering to God and admitting that our lives are out of control, we find that we begin to come out of a condition known as denial. Denial is a common coping mechanism that we employ in an effort to keep ourselves safe emotionally. If we can pretend a problem doesn't exist, we don't have to deal with it and it can't harm us. Of course, the opposite is true. Denial can hurt us badly by numbing our emotions and keeping us from dealing with problems until they become critical.

Denial manifests itself in many ways. Some people turn to shopping, sex, drugs, overeating, inappropriate images, risky relationships—anything that can keep us from facing reality. These problems are then added to the underlying problem, and we are in even more trouble than we were before.

In the book of John, we read that Jesus had lost a friend, a man named Lazarus. This man and his two sisters frequently invited Jesus to stay in their home when he was in the area. When Jesus arrived, the two women were crying. He didn't ask them to deny their grief and pretend they weren't grieving. Just the opposite. He wept along with them. It's always better to face things squarely than to sweep them under the rug.

PRAYER

Father, it's natural to want to sweep the bad stuff under the rug, but that's not how you taught me to deal with unwelcome circumstances. Thank you for teaching me to deal with things squarely. In Jesus' name, Amen.

The Sixth Step

Humble yourselves before the Lord,
and he will lift you up.

JAMES 4:10

In some recovery material, Step 6 has been referred to as the step that separates the men from the boys. Make no mistake, it also separates the women from the girls. One of the reasons the sixth step is so daunting is that it asks us to allow God to remove *all* our defects of character. Not *some*, but *all*!

Step 6: We were entirely ready to have God remove all these defects of character.

Most of us would be more than willing to have certain character defects go away—and the sooner the better! But let's face it, there are others that are hard to give up. I'm an alcoholic, but there came a time in my life, a moment of clarity, when I knew I had hit bottom and was ready to stop drinking. But was I ready to stop lying? Stop being greedy? Was I ready to let go of resentments, impatience, selfishness? I had been indulging these things for a long time. Like weeds in a garden, the roots went deep! Sure, I could see what needed to be done, but could I allow the changes to occur? Each of us must find the answers to these questions.

That place between recognition and willingness can be filled with fear, and fear can trigger old dependencies. It's essential that we accept God's help throughout this step.

PRAYER

Father, I admit I am fearful and anxious about dealing with my character defects. I ask again for your help as I take this important step. In Jesus' name, Amen.

Hurt People, Hurt People

*Let us fix our eyes on Jesus, the author
and perfecter of our faith, who for the
joy set before him endured the cross.*

HEBREWS 12:2

In recovery we hear that "hurt people, hurt people." We've all experienced this, and sometimes, we see it happen to others. It's heartbreaking. School shootings, for example, are a grotesque display of true evil that has brought heartbreak and pain to so many lives. How are we to deal with such deep pain? Where is the hope in a tragedy such as this?

The answer is that we have no hope apart from Christ. Without him, such tragedies just spawn more hurting people who go on to lash out at others in a futile effort to quench their own pain. Jesus is the only source of comfort and light capable of guiding us through our pain to a better place.

When our hearts are breaking and we have questions swirling around in our heads—questions we fear have no answers—God invites us to come and talk it out with him. Many of the answers may be past our comprehension, but knowing the answers are safe with him allows us to hand our questions—burdens too great for us to bear—over to him. God cares about everything that concerns us, everything that grieves our hearts. In the midst of the darkness, he is our hope, the one we can trust.

PRAYER

Lord, my heart is breaking as I see hurting people hurting people all around me. Help me to leave my unanswered questions with you. In Jesus' name, Amen.

The Seventh Step

If we confess our sins, he is faithful and
just and will forgive us our sins and
purify us from all unrighteousness.

1 JOHN 1:9

O nce we ask God to remove our character defects and shortcomings, we begin a journey that will lead us to new freedom from our past. We shouldn't look for perfection, but instead rejoice in steady progress. In other words, patient improvement. God has promised to keep right on helping us until the work within us is finished (Philippians 1:6). He's in it for the long haul.

Step 7: We humbly asked him to remove all our
shortcomings.

If we cling to self-reliance, we will never go beyond this step, but victory is ensured as long as we truly place our reliance on God. We must voluntarily submit to every change he wants us to make in our lives and humbly ask him to remove every shortcoming. We must be fully committed to allowing God to be the life-changer!

We are not the "how" and "when" committee. We are the preparation committee—all we have to do is be ready! And if there is suffering in the process, it won't be wasted. God will use everything, even tears of pain, to turn our weaknesses into strengths. All we need to do is humbly ask for his help and be willing to follow his lead. He won't quit until the job is done!

PRAYER

My loving Father, help me prepare my heart for the change you are bringing to my life. I trust that you will continue your work in me until all my weaknesses have been turned into strengths. In Jesus' name, Amen.

A Light to My Feet

Your word is a lamp to my feet and a light for my path.

PSALM 119:105

As we walk the road to recovery, we often find ourselves wondering if we are on the right path. There are times when it seems we have far more questions than answers. Am I going the right way? Is this working? Should I keep going, or should I turn around and go back? Does anyone notice how much I've changed?

When we are faced with these questions, we need to go first to God's Word, the Bible. Our accountability partners and sponsors can offer insight, but only God has the truth we need to make our recovery succeed. In the book of Psalms, we read that God's Word serves as a light to our feet. All of us have experienced times of real darkness—no flashlights, no streetlights. When we walk in a world full of darkness, we need a lamp to show us where to take our next step.

The Bible is that lamp. Step-by-step God leads us, showing us what to do. He may not show us his entire plan for our lives, but through his Word, he shows us one step at a time. The truth is, we don't need all the answers. Not right now anyway. Instead, we need just enough light for our feet.

PRAYER

Thank you, Lord, for giving me your Word to light the path along my journey. Help me to take one step at a time. In Jesus' name, Amen.

The Eighth Step

"Do to others as you would have them do to you."

LUKE 6:31

In Step 6, we asked God to clear out the roots of our character defects. Then in Step 7, we humbled ourselves, freeing ourselves from pride. Now that we're free, God can begin to change us, as he has promised. Now we're ready for the next step.

Step 8: We made a list of all persons we had harmed and became willing to make amends to them all.

God forgave us for all our wrongs, all our sins. But we still have to deal with the trail of wreckage those wrongs have strewn along the path. That means making amends and restitution. As we reconcile ourselves with others, we are able to shed the shame and guilt that is impeding the progress of our recovery.

The list of those we've harmed should be both comprehensive and complete. No rationalizations, no hedging. That means old resentments have to come into the light, pride banished, and the truth embraced. It won't be easy, but it will be worth it. It does no good to bury the past. Some old dog will dig up the bones and bring them back to our door. The past must be dealt with and cleared, so that our new lives can be built on a firm foundation.

PRAYER

Lord, guide me as I make my list. I realize it will mean reliving painful memories, but, with your help and your presence here with me, I'm ready to do my best. In Jesus' name, Amen.

Positive Habits

"When an evil spirit comes out of a man, it goes through arid places seeking rest and does not find it. Then it says, 'I will return to the house I left.' When it arrives, it finds the house unoccupied, swept clean and put in order. Then it goes and takes with it seven other spirits more wicked than itself, and they go in and live there."

MATTHEW 12:43–45

We begin recovery by focusing our attention on ridding ourselves of negative habits. We then learn that lasting change comes only through God's power. As the days pass, we became more and more free from our old hurts, hang-ups, and habits. We make fewer poor, unhealthy choices, and we grow closer to the one and only Higher Power—Jesus Christ. Reaching that point in our recovery is a great accomplishment as well as a dangerous place to be. It's a mistake to say we have arrived. Unless we keep moving forward, we risk relapse, which can actually leave us worse off than when we began.

We must always be hard at work making positive choices and adding new, healthy habits to our daily lives. And even more important, we must work to keep our relationship with God fresh and vibrant. We can do this by reserving a daily time with God for self-examination, Bible reading, and prayer. The more we know God and his will for our lives, the more we fortify ourselves against relapse, strengthen our relationship with God, and become empowered to reach out to others through our words and example.

PRAYER

Holy Father, thank you for rescuing me from my mess and empowering me to hold on to my freedom. In Jesus' name, Amen.

The Ninth Step

"Therefore, if you are offering your gift at the altar and there remember that your brother has something against you, leave your gift there in front of the altar. First go and be reconciled to your brother; then come and offer your gift."

MATTHEW 5:23–24

In Step 8, we evaluated all our relationships. We became willing to offer forgiveness to those who have hurt us and to make amends for the harm that we have done to others. We agreed to do this without expecting anything in return. Now we must walk the talk.

Step 9: We made direct amends to such people whenever possible, except when to do so would injure them or others.

As we grow in faith and pursue recovery, we want to follow the example Jesus set. As we get to know him better, we want to model his teachings and his ways. We want to become more like him. If we are to implement Step 9 to the best of our ability, we must learn to model God's grace.

Grace is a gift. It cannot be bought. We know this because God has given it to us without expecting anything in return. When we offer our amends in the same way, we are offering a gift to those we have harmed. On a human level, we might not feel that some of these people deserve such a gift, but neither do we deserve any of God's gifts to us. God showers us with his grace, and his strength is ours as we go and do likewise.

PRAYER

Father God, I need your help as I set out to make amends with those I've harmed. Endow me, Lord, with wisdom and courage to do what has to be done. In Jesus' name, Amen.

Be Still and Know

Be still, and know that I am God.

PSALM 46:10

I've noticed that there is always a temptation to be going somewhere, doing something. We fill our calendars, to-do lists, and appointment books to overflowing. A successful day is marked by going to bed exhausted, only to wake to another day just as full as the last. Somehow that doesn't seem right to me. How are we supposed to hear God's voice if we are always racing through life? I think that's what God is talking about when he says, "Be still!"

Why don't we all try being still together, beginning with a prayer? Let's tell God that for the next few minutes, we aren't going anywhere or doing anything. We are just going to be still and wait in his presence. Now, let's clear our minds of all the questions and thoughts about our day. We want to quiet ourselves before him as well. Maybe he'll speak to us this time and maybe he won't, but at the very least, quiet time with him will refresh and uplift us.

From now on, let's meet with God in stillness every day. It might take some getting used to, but once it has become a habit, a healthy one, God is sure to make himself known. Sitting and being still before him may not sound exciting, but every time we are in God's presence, listening for his voice, we are right where he wants us. That's a very exciting place to be.

PRAYER

I'm here, Father, waiting in your presence. It's so peaceful here. In Jesus' name, Amen.

The Tenth Step

So, if you think you are standing firm,
be careful that you don't fall!

1 CORINTHIANS 10:12

If we are wrong . . . wait, change that . . . *when* we are wrong! No matter how long we've been in a recovery program, we are still going to make mistakes. And when we do, we need to promptly make our amends. We all need to work Step 10 into our lives on a daily basis.

> *Step 10: We continued to take personal inventory and when we were wrong, promptly admitted it.*

I recently received this e-mail from a Celebrate Recovery ministry leader:

> I'm pretty disappointed. I understand that you get a lot of e-mails asking you to speak, and it would be difficult to speak at all of them, but I really thought someone would reply back. It wouldn't even have mattered if someone

answered for you. It would just be nice to know my e-mail was read. May God continue to bless you and Celebrate Recovery.

Within thirty minutes I e-mailed my amends:

Thank you for your e-mail. I'm so sorry I let you down. We were checking to see if the date was available, and somehow it got lost in the process. I apologize for any inconvenience I caused. Congratulations on your four years. I wish I could have been there. In his steps, Pastor John

I am sharing these notes to show that I'm still using the program every day to the best of my ability. That is how we stay dependent on God's power.

PRAYER

Father, thank you for letting me know when I'm wrong. And thank you for giving me the courage to make amends. In Jesus' name, Amen.

Iron Sharpens Iron

As iron sharpens iron, so one person sharpens another.

PROVERBS 27:17

I was working when I heard someone crying. I went out to check and discovered that it was one of our volunteers. Her husband is an addict, and she's going through some tough times with her daughter as well. She had just gotten off the phone with someone who has been dealing with a lot of the same issues. All at once, she felt joy for the victories she's seen and deep sadness for the battles that still lay ahead.

This volunteer has gone through her own personal hell. Her husband's addiction and her daughter's rebellion have caused her deep grief. But working through the Celebrate Recovery principles has helped her to find victory for herself and learn that she can change only herself—no one else. So that day, when she called the parents of a troubled teen to talk about recovery options, she was able to encourage them. She knew they needed recovery as much as anyone. She sharpened and encouraged them. God used her personal pain to help others.

We all have a story. We've known pain. We've worked through difficult issues. God can use our experiences to sharpen others if we will let him.

PRAYER

Dear Father, thank you for turning my pain into blessing by using it to challenge and encourage others. In Jesus' name, Amen.

The Eleventh Step

Let the word of Christ dwell in you richly.

COLOSSIANS 3:16 NKJV

We have taken ten steps now on our road to recovery. We are living out the decision we made in Step 3. We are growing in our understanding of God, improving our conscious contact with him, and conducting honest inventories on a regular basis.

Step 11: We sought through prayer and meditation to improve our conscious contact with God, praying only for knowledge of his will for us and power to carry that out.

As our relationship with God deepens, it's important for us to reserve time apart with him every day. During this time, we learn to focus on him through prayer and meditation. When I say *prayer*, I simply mean talking to God. For me, meditation is just getting quiet so we can hear what God is saying. I don't get into some yoga-type position or murmur, "Om, om, om." I simply focus on and think about God, a certain verse from Scripture, or maybe even just one or two words. This morning I spent ten or fifteen minutes just focusing on one word: *gratitude*.

Talking to God and listening for his voice is the best way to silence those old familiar friends of past dysfunction. They want to interrupt my quiet time with God because they don't want me to hear him say that I have great worth, that I bring him joy. I know that my talks with God strengthen me to meet the challenges of each day.

PRAYER

Dear Father, thank you for always being there for me, always listening, loving, teaching, strengthening, and encouraging. In Jesus' name, Amen.

The Twelfth Step

*Brothers, if someone is caught in a sin, you who
are spiritual should restore him gently. But
watch yourself, or you also may be tempted.*

GALATIANS 6:1

Modern technology is something else! Take, for example, an old, beat-up soft drink can: dirty, dented, with holes in it. A few years ago, it would have been thrown into the garbage and deemed useless, of no value. But these days, it can be recycled, melted down, purified, and made into a new can, shiny and clean, something that can be used again.

*Step 12: Having had a spiritual experience as the
result of these steps, we try to carry this message to
others and to practice these principles in all our affairs.*

Our pain can be recycled as well! When we allow God's purifying fire to work on our hurts, hang-ups, and habits, they can be melted down and used again in a positive way. Recycling our pain in this way—in God's way—can help others see that the recovery principles will work for them just as they've worked for us. It can serve to encourage others that they too will come through the darkness into Christ's glorious freedom and light.

At Celebrate Recovery, we know that pain has value, as do the people who experience it. Our pain has meaning because it has been transformed by God's hand. We have purpose because he has turned our lives around.

PRAYER

Dear Jesus, thank you for redeeming my pain. Thank you for transforming it for your glory and for the sake of those who need to know that recovery is possible. In Jesus' name, Amen.

What Makes It Work?

Praise be to the God and Father of our Lord Jesus
Christ, the Father of compassion and the God of
all comfort, who comforts us in all our troubles, so
that we can comfort those in any trouble with the
comfort we ourselves have received from God.

2 CORINTHIANS 1:3–4

Benjamin Franklin said, "Tell me and I forget. Teach me and I remember. Involve me and I learn." That's a big reason why Celebrate Recovery works. The program acknowledges that just listening—tell me and I forget—isn't enough. Even remembering—teach me and I remember—won't do the trick. The only way to be successful is by doing—involve me and I learn.

We all begin at the same place: acknowledging that we are completely dependent on God's power, surrendered to his will, and committed to working the program's principles and steps. Once we've learned how to break free from our hurts, hang-ups, and habits, we must get involved and start giving back what we have learned by helping others.

As stated in Step 8, we are to yield ourselves to God to be used to bring this Good News to others, both by our example and our words. Step 12 requires that once we have had a spiritual experience as a result of taking the program's steps, we are to carry that message to others and practice those principles in all our affairs.

Healing and wholeness are more than a state of being. They are also a state of doing as we constantly renew our commitment and demonstrate our thankfulness by giving to others.

PRAYER

Heavenly Father, help me once again to acknowledge my dependence on you and confirm that commitment by sharing with others. In Jesus' name, Amen.

Taking Action

*I urge you, brothers, in view of God's mercy, to offer
your bodies as living sacrifices, holy and pleasing
to God—this is your spiritual act of worship.*

ROMANS 12:1

Even after we admit that our lives are out of control,
we can still get stuck in a cycle of failure that keeps
us bound by guilt, anger, fear, and depression. How do
we get past those old, familiar, negative barriers that keep
us from freedom and wholeness? We do that by taking
action. Making a choice requires action.

The trouble is that most of us don't like making deci-
sions. We would rather just follow the crowd because
that's easier than stepping out and doing what we know is
right. We procrastinate about making commitments that
will allow change to occur, clinging instead to our hurts,
hang-ups, and habits. We forget that failing to choose is in
itself a choice.

All we really need is the willingness to make a decision. God will help us with the rest. Why should we

continue to struggle when the road to relief, wholeness, freedom, and a new life is just one choice away? That's where all true recovery begins, with action. And that action can open up a whole new way of living.

PRAYER

Father, I'm tired of fighting to stay alive, wondering if there is any hope for me. I am taking action right now, asking for your help and asking for the strength to pursue recovery. In Jesus' name, Amen.

The *Celebrate Recovery Bible* offers everyone hope, encouragement, and the empowerment to rise above their hurts, hang-ups, and habits. This life-changing Bible is based on the proven and successful Celebrate Recovery program developed by John Baker and Rick Warren.

With features based on eight principles Jesus voiced in his Sermon on the Mount, this insightful Bible is for anyone struggling with the circumstances of their lives and the habits they are trying to control.